534.078   122484
Woo   Wood,Robert W.

Sound Fundamentals

Other books in the FUNdamental Series
Heat FUNdamentals
Light FUNdamentals
Electricity and Magnetism FUNdamentals
Mechanics FUNdamentals

SOUND

FUNDAMENTALS

FUNtastic Science Activities for Kids

Robert W. Wood

Illustrated by Rick Brown

Chelsea House Publishers

Philadelphia

Library of Congress Cataloging-in-Publication Data

Wood, Robert W., 1933-
    Sound fundamentals : funtastic science activities for kids /
Robert W. Wood : Illustrated by Rick Brown.
       p.   cm. — (FUNdamentals)
Originally published: New York : McGraw-Hill, 1997.
Includes index.
    Summary: Provides instructions for over twenty-five simple
activities involving sound, including creating thunder, making music,
in a bottle, and exploring echoes.
    ISBN 0-7910-4840-3 (hardcover)
    1. Sound—Experiments—Juvenile literature. [1. Sound-
-Experiments. 2. Experiments.] I. Brown, Rick, 1946- ill.
II. Title. III. Series: FUNdamentals (Philadelphia, Pa.)
QC225.5.W68 1997b
534'.078—dc21
                                                  97-30096
                                                     CIP
                                                     AC

CONTENTS

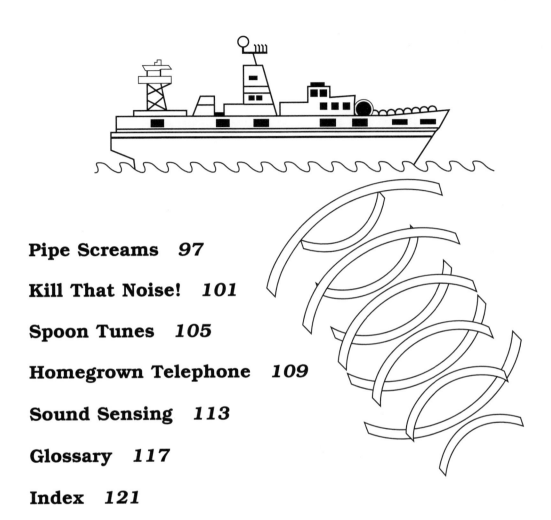

INTRO

Sound is all around us: the wind whistles or howls, a dog barks, people speak on the street, and birds sing. But where does sound come from? And how do we hear it?

The study of sound includes a lot of different areas. Scientists study sound and the effects it has on people. When designing buildings, engineers must understand how sound behaves. Hospitals and libraries must have quiet areas, while auditoriums are built to carry sound to people in the audience. Composers and musicians understand how sounds are used to make us react a certain way and to stir our emotions. Linguists study how we use sounds to communicate.

Sound is very important to our daily lives. It can wake us up in the morning. It can entertain us or warn us of danger. It can even tell us what time it is, as when a clock chimes. Visually impaired people rely on sound in many ways that sighted people do not. People with hearing impairments must use their other senses to go about their routines.

The activities in this book present the basics for understanding how sound works and some of the ways humans influence sound. These experiments are easy to do, yet they demonstrate important principles about sound. Each experiment begins with "Your Challenge," which tells you what you are trying to accomplish. A materials list of things found around the house follows. Step-by-step procedures are given, along with illustrations of many of the steps. "What Happened" explains what the experiment showed and adds a few questions to discuss the experiment further. Each experiment also has a section called "Check This Out," which includes more fun things to do with sound. The experiments end with fascinating and amusing facts.

Be sure to read "Safety Stuff" before you begin any experiment. It tells you what safety precautions you should take. It also tells you whether you should have a teacher or another adult help you. Keep safety in mind, keep your ears open, and you will have a fun and exciting time discovering sound.

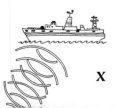

SAFETY STUFF

Science experiments can be fun and exciting, but safety should always be considered. Parents and teachers are encouraged to participate with their children and students.

 Look over the steps before beginning any experiment. You will notice that some steps are preceded by a caution symbol like the one next to this paragraph. This symbol means that you should use extra safety precautions or that the experiment requires adult supervision.

Materials or tools used in some experiments could be dangerous in young hands. Adult supervision is recommended whenever the caution symbol appears. Children need to be taught about the care and handling of sharp tools or combustible or toxic materials and how to protect surfaces. Also, extreme caution must be exercised around any open flame.

Use common sense and make safety the priority, and you will have a safe and fun experience!

Try this experiment to make salt dance.

GOOD VIBRATIONS

YOUR CHALLENGE

To observe the results of sound vibrations.

DO THIS

1   Stretch a sheet of plastic food wrap over the opening of one of the coffee cans. Fasten it in place with the rubber band.

2   Gently pull down on the free edges of the plastic wrap to smooth the area stretched over the top of the can. The can will be a type of drum. (Figure 1-1)

3   Sprinkle a little salt on the stretched plastic.

4   Hold the remaining coffee can about 30 cm (12 inches) directly above the first can. Point the opening at the grains of salt, and tap the bottom of the can with the spoon. What sounds do you hear? What happens to the grains of salt? (Figure 1-2)

YOU NEED

Two empty coffee cans without lids

Plastic food wrap about 30 cm (12 inches) square

Rubber band

Salt

Wooden spoon

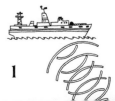

1

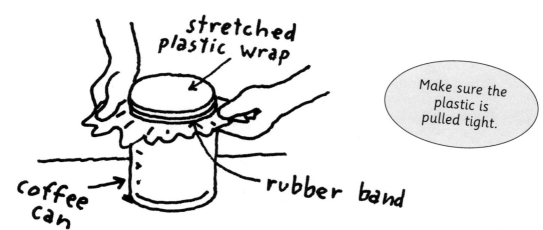

stretched plastic wrap

Make sure the plastic is pulled tight.

coffee can

rubber band

Figure 1-1

Tap the coffee can with a spoon.

A little drumroll, please...

Salt

Figure 1-2

WHAT HAPPENED?

All sound is created by something vibrating. When something vibrates, it moves back and forth. When you tap the coffee can, the can continues to vibrate for a split second. At the same time, the air around the can

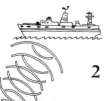

2

vibrates too. These vibrations are *sound waves*. When the sound waves reach the plastic, they cause the plastic to vibrate and the salt to "dance." When these same sound waves reach your ear, you hear the tapping sound. (Figure 1-3)

The sound waves travel to the other can and to your ear.

Figure 1-3

Q: Why did the little boy throw the drum down the hill?
A: He wanted to hear a drumroll!

How do you think a violin makes music? How about a piano?

Check This Out

Sound needs a medium, such as air, to carry it. Over two thousand years ago, Aristotle guessed that sound couldn't be produced in a *vacuum*, or an enclosure where all the air has been removed. But not until the 17th century did the Irish scientist Robert Boyle prove Aristotle's theory. He set a ticking clock in an enclosure and removed all the air with a specially designed pump. Sure enough, as the air was removed, the ticking became fainter and fainter until no sound at all could be heard.

★ Drums are found in practically every culture and have existed since at least 600 BC.

★ Since outer space is a vacuum, astronauts on the moon can't hear each other speak. They must talk to each other through radios. Only if they touch helmets can they speak directly to one another. This permits sufficient vibrations so that sound waves can be transmitted through the materials of their helmets. (Figure 1-4)

Figure 1-4

What would sound waves
look like if you could see them?

CATCH A WAVE!

YOUR CHALLENGE

To observe a pattern of waves similar to sound waves.

DO THIS

1 Place the pan on a level surface and fill it with about 2 or
   3 cm (1 inch) of water. Let the water stand until the
   surface is smooth and flat.

2 Use the medicine dropper to drop a single drop of water
   into the pan near one end. (Figure 2-1)

3 Observe the ripples. What happens to them? How long do
   they last?

4 Try dropping another drop of water near one of the
   existing ripples. Now what do the ripples do? Can you
   explain the differences?

YOU NEED

Large baking pan

Water

Medicine dropper

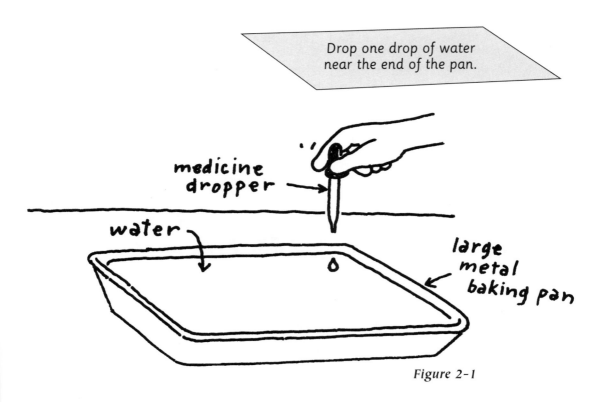

Drop one drop of water near the end of the pan.

medicine dropper

water

large metal baking pan

Figure 2-1

WHAT HAPPENED?

When a vibrating object produces a sound, it causes the nearby air molecules to move back and forth. This forces the surrounding air molecules to move back and forth as well. The back-and-forth movement forms waves of vibrating air molecules called *sound waves*. These waves spread out through the air in all directions. If the waves happen to reach someone's ear, they cause that person's eardrum to start vibrating, and the waves are detected by the brain as sound.

Sound, then, depends on a vibrating source, air to carry the waves of sound, and an ear to receive them. If you could see sound waves and were able to look down into a room shaped like the pan, you would see sound waves behaving like the ripples of water. The point where the drop hit the water would be where someone was speaking.

The ear is made up of the *outer ear*, or the part we can see plus the ear canal, the *middle ear*, and the *inner ear*. The *eardrum* is a thin skin, or *membrane*, that separates the middle ear from the outer ear. We hear sounds because when sound waves strike the eardrum, the eardrum vibrates. The vibrations become stronger in the middle ear and are changed into electrical signals. Nerves carry the signals to the brain, and the brain "unscrambles the message" and tells you what you are hearing. (Figure 2-2)

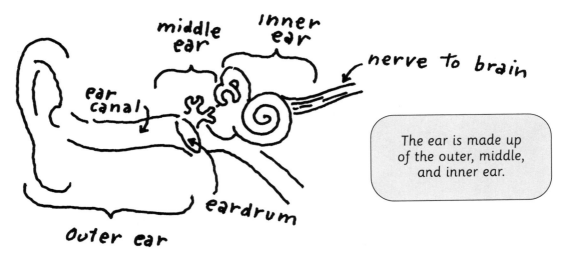

The ear is made up of the outer, middle, and inner ear.

Figure 2-2

Check This Out

Have you ever heard the question, "If a tree falls in a forest, but no one is there to hear it, does it make a sound?" The answer depends on how sound is defined. If you believe that wherever there are sound waves, there is sound, the answer would be yes. But if you believe that sound is a sensation in the ear, then the answer would be no. Since there is no receiver, or ear, to detect the sound, there would be no sound.

★ Eardrums are not located on the sides of the head in all creatures. For instance, a frog's eardrums are located behind its eyes. The eardrums of a grasshopper are on its abdomen, just behind its legs. (Figure 2-3)

★ Some creatures, like chameleons, have no eardrums.

Figure 2-3

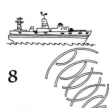

Ever wonder why you don't hear
thunder at the same time as lightning?
You'll learn why in a flash!

FLASH
AND CRASH

YOUR CHALLENGE

To use the speed of a sound to measure distance.

DO THIS

1 Watch for a flash of lightning. The instant you see the flash, start counting the seconds on the watch until you hear the thunder. (If a watch is not handy, simply count "thousand-one, thousand-two, thousand-three," and so on to represent each second.) (Figure 3-1)

2 Sound travels through the air at about 335.5 meters (1,100 feet) per second. Multiply this speed times the number of seconds between the lightning and thunder. This will tell you how far away the lightning is.

YOU NEED

Thunderstorm

Watch with a second hand

Figure 3-1

WHAT HAPPENED?

The reason that lightning and thunder don't seem to happen at the same time is that the speed of light is a million times faster than the speed of sound. This means that you see the lightning almost at the instant it strikes. However, you don't hear the thunder until a little later because it takes longer for the sound to reach your ears. This causes a delay between the "flash" and the "crash."

The length of time it takes the sound of the thunder to reach you tells you how far you are from the lightning. For instance, say it takes five seconds for the thunder to reach you. To get the distance in meters, multiply 5 times 335.5 meters. For the distance in feet, multiply 5 times 1,100 feet. The distance will be about 1,677 meters, or 5,500 feet. This means that the lightning is a little over 1.609 kilometers (1 mile) away.

CHECK THIS OUT

The next time you go to a fireworks display, see if you notice a delay between the display and the "boom." Do you think the delay is caused by the speed of light versus the speed of sound? Could you calculate how far the rockets are being set off by timing the flash of light and the boom, as you did with lightning and thunder? (Figure 3-2)

Another way you can observe this principle is while watching a baseball game. Notice when you see the bat make contact with the ball and when you hear the "crack."

Figure 3-2

GUESS WHAT?

⭐ *When an aircraft goes faster than the speed of sound, called* Mach 1 *or supersonic speed, it produces a special sound wave called a* sonic boom. *The sonic boom doesn't just happen when the sound barrier is crossed, but remains with the aircraft as long as the aircraft is at supersonic speeds. This means that the boom also follows the aircraft.*

⭐ *For over 20 years, the Concorde, a supersonic aircraft, has been carrying passengers across the Atlantic at twice the speed of sound, or Mach 2.*

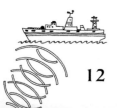

This one will have you thunderstruck!

EVER WONDER ABOUT THUNDER?

YOUR CHALLENGE

To discover what happens when air is suddenly compressed.

DO THIS

1   Blow up the paper bag and twist the opening, making a seal to trap the air.

2   Pop the bag between your hands. What do you hear? (Figure 4-1)

YOU NEED

Paper bag

Pop the bag.

paper bag

Try a plastic bag for a different sound.

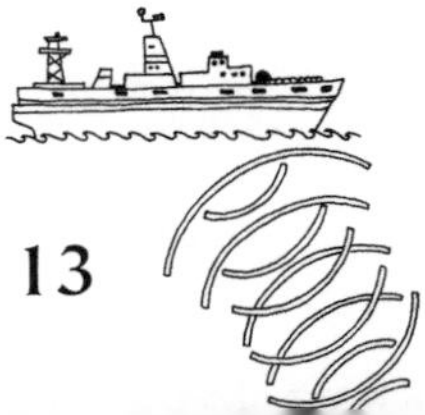

Figure 4-1

13

What Happened?

When lightning strikes, the bolt generates tremendous amounts of heat. This heat *compresses*, or squeezes together, the surrounding air, leaving a low-pressure area where the bolt traveled. Simply put, the lightning bolt pushes the air out and makes a hole in the atmosphere. You hear the bang when the air comes back together to normal pressure.

So even though thunder and lightning can be scary, you can think of it as a giant paper bag being popped in the sky!

Check This Out

The sound that thunder makes is a sonic boom. Sonic booms happen when an object, such as the heat from a lightning bolt, tries to move through the air faster than the speed of sound. Another example of a sonic boom is the cracking sound a bullwhip makes. In fact, whips can reach speeds of 700 miles an hour. You can imitate this sound with a leather belt. Take the belt (be sure to ask the owner first), and fold it in half. Hold the belt tightly with your hands at each end. Bring your fists together so that the halves of the belt separate. Now rapidly pull your hands apart so that the halves slap together. The sound you create resembles a cracking whip.

Figure 4-2

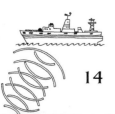

GUESS WHAT?

⭐ Earth scientists, called geophysicists, set off small explosions to generate sound waves that can indicate underground mineral deposits. Sound waves that travel through the earth are called seismic waves.

⭐ The vocal cords in all mammals and in some reptiles and amphibians are contained in the voice box, or larynx. Birds do not have a larynx. They produce sounds by vibrating membranes (thin sheets of skin) at the lower end of the windpipe in an organ called the syrinx. The shape of this structure and the muscles that operate the membranes vary with different families of birds. This difference produces the variety of songs we enjoy. (Figure 4-2)

This one sounds interesting!

FEELING THE FREQUENCY

YOUR CHALLENGE

To observe the frequencies of different sounds.

DO THIS

1 Place the metal meter or yardstick about halfway over the edge of the table. Press down firmly and thump the extended end with your finger. What do you observe? (Figure 5-1)

2 Repeat the steps, gradually sticking more of the metal stick over the edge. How does this change the sound?

3 Try the same experiment with the wooden meter or yardstick. How do the sounds compare?

YOU NEED

Table

Metal meter or yardstick

Wooden meter or yardstick

Large rubber band

Small rubber band

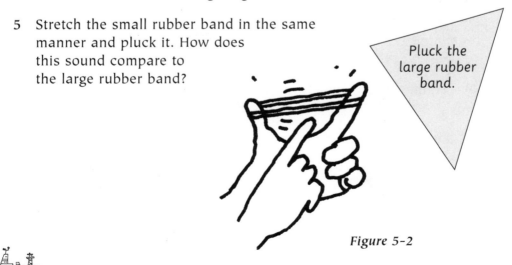

Thump the metal yardstick. Hum along if you like.

rubber band

yard stick

Figure 5-1

4   Now stretch the large rubber band between your thumb and a finger. Pluck it to start it vibrating. (Figure 5-2)

5   Stretch the small rubber band in the same manner and pluck it. How does this sound compare to the large rubber band?

Pluck the large rubber band.

Figure 5-2

What Happened?

The sounds produced by the metal stick, the wooden stick, and the rubber bands were caused by vibrations. How fast something vibrates determines the frequency. The *frequency* of a sound is the number of times an object, or the sound waves it produces, vibrates in a second. Which had the higher frequency, the metal or wooden stick? Did how far they extended over the table affect the frequency? How did the frequency of the object compare to the sound it produced?

Of the two rubber bands, which had the higher frequency? How did the sounds compare? What does this tell you about how frequency affects sound?

Could what you observed with the rubber bands help you explain why a grown-up's voice is usually lower than a child's? Here's a hint: Would you expect the vocal chords of a tall person to be longer or shorter than a short person?

Frequency is measured in units called *hertz*, which are the number of sound-wave cycles that pass by a given point each second. Humans can hear sounds with frequencies between about 20 and 20,000 hertz. Hertz also describes *pitch*, or how high or low a sound is.

Check This Out

Units called *decibels* (abbreviated dB) measure the amount of pressure exerted on the eardrum from a sound vibration. In other words, decibels measure loudness. A subway train produces sounds of about 90 decibels, and a rock band produces sounds of about 110 decibels. A sound of about 140 decibels starts to produce pain. Here are the decibel readings of some familiar sounds:

- Ordinary breathing: 10 dB
- Talking: 30 to 60 dB
- Vacuum cleaner: 60 to 80 dB
- Traffic, motorcycles, trains, subway cars: 70 to 90 dB
- Thunder: 95 to 115 dB
- Jet takeoff: 120 to 140 dB

Guess What?

★ *The ear first evolved as an organ of balance, and fish still use this primitive organ. Only later in humans and higher vertebrates did the ear become a structure of hearing as well as balance. (Figure 5-3)*

★ *A young person may be able to hear 20,000-hertz sounds, but by the time this same person reaches middle age, he or she may be unable to hear sounds with frequencies above 12,000 to 14,000 hertz.*

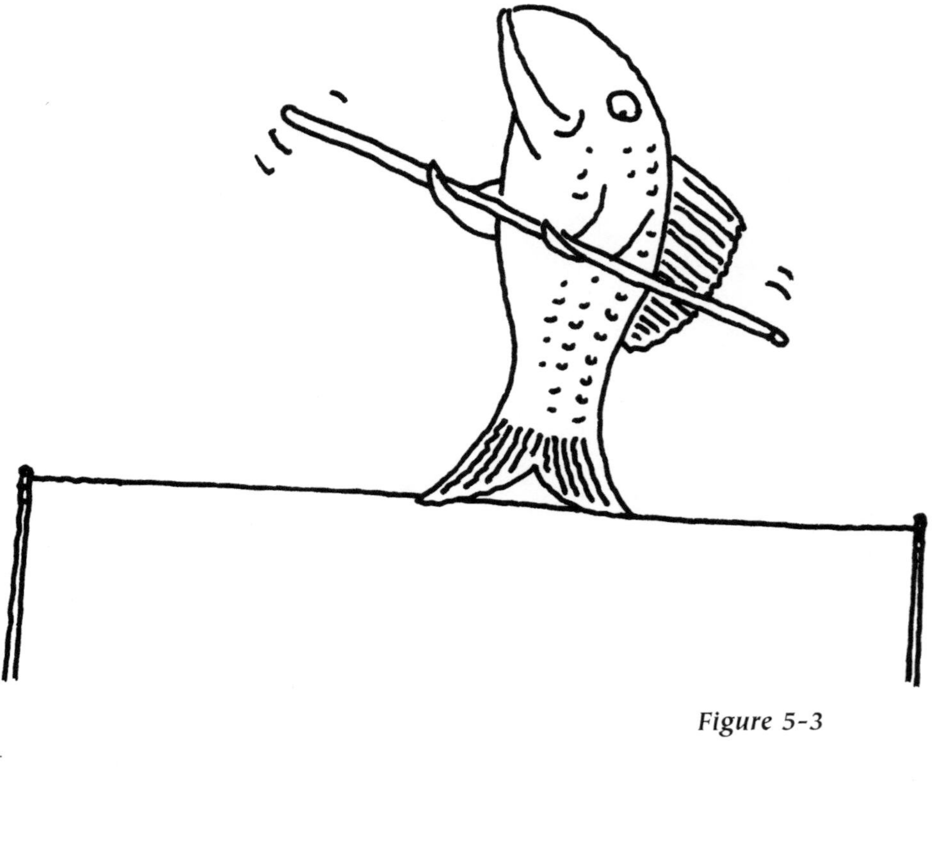

Figure 5-3

VIBRATING VOCALS

You don't need any materials for this one.

YOUR CHALLENGE

To observe how we produce speech.

DO THIS

1   Place your hand at the front part of your throat and speak or hum a tune. What do you feel? (Figure 6-1)

2   Continue humming and press in and out softly with your fingers. What happens to the sound?

Touch your throat with your fingertips. Don't worry...it's supposed to feel a little weird.

YOU NEED

Just yourself

Figure 6-1

21

What Happened?

Two small flaps of tissue in the upper part of the windpipe are the vocal cords that produce the sound. When we inhale, the vocal cords move outward toward the walls of the windpipe. When sound is to be produced, the cords move in and the muscles contract to make the cords taut. Air exhaled from the lungs passes over the cords and causes them to vibrate. When you press in, you are causing the cords to become tighter, so the pitch becomes higher.

Have you ever noticed that your voice becomes higher when you are excited about something? Why do you think this happens?

Check This Out

Try humming, speaking, and singing through the cage of a moving fan. (Be careful not to get too close to the blades, though!) Why do you think your voice sounds like it does?

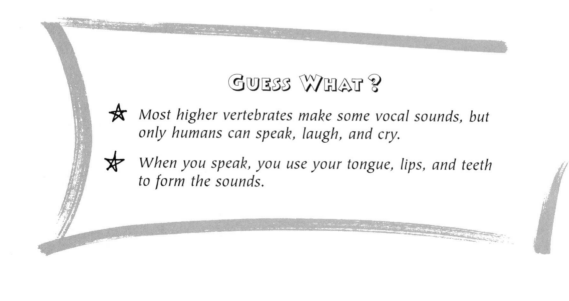

Guess What?

★ Most higher vertebrates make some vocal sounds, but only humans can speak, laugh, and cry.

★ When you speak, you use your tongue, lips, and teeth to form the sounds.

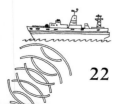

Next time a grown-up tells you the music
you're listening to sounds like noise,
you can explain the difference!

Is That Noise or Is That Music?

Your Challenge

To discover the differences between noise and music.

Do This

1 Blow up the balloon and pinch the opening between your thumb and finger.

2 Hold the balloon under one arm and against your side. Make sure the opening is pointing toward the front.

3 Stretch the opening of the balloon from side to side while you release the air. What do you hear? (Figure 7-1)

4 Stretch the opening farther and press the balloon with your arm as you release more air. What happens to the sound?

balloon

Pull the opening so a little air comes out. You can make lots of funny sounds.

Figure 7-1

5 Try varying the pressure and the size of the opening to produce vibrations in a regular pattern. Now what do you hear?

WHAT HAPPENED?

When air is forced through the stretched opening, the rubber vibrates and the air comes out in a series of waves. Usually, these are in an irregular wave pattern. This irregular pattern produces noise. If you were able to produce sound waves in a regular pattern, it produced musical sounds. The difference between noise and music is in the wave patterns.

Can you think of a musical instrument that uses the same principle you demonstrated with the balloon to create sounds?

CHECK THIS OUT

Noise can also be defined as unwanted sound. But whether the sound is unwanted is determined by the listener. A train, for example, might be very noisy, but people who live close to the train tracks might not even notice the sound because they are accustomed to it. Likewise, someone who lives in the city and is used to the hustle and bustle might find the sounds in the country to be irritating. Noise, then, can be determined by its loudness, its frequency, and whether the noise is unusual to the listener.

GUESS WHAT?

★ *Prolonged loud noises may lead to a temporary or permanent hearing loss.*

★ *The creaking sounds you sometimes hear at night are caused by your home "settling." No building is ever completely at rest. Soil beneath the foundation buckles, and the lumber used in the frame shrinks when it gets wet and expands when it dries. Also, the roof over your head expands in the warm, midday sun and shrinks at night when it's cooler. In fact, the entire building grows larger in warm weather and smaller in cold weather. (Figure 7-2)*

Figure 7-2

If you have a dog, see how he reacts to your dog-bark noisemaker!

BARKING DOGS

YOUR CHALLENGE

To produce sounds similar to a barking dog.

DO THIS

⚠️ 1 Thoroughly rinse the plastic jug. With scissors, carefully cut off the bottom of the jug, or have an adult do it.

2 Dry the inside of the jug to ensure better sound quality.

⚠️ 3 Have an adult use a hammer and nail to make a small hole in the lid.

4 Thread one end of the cord through the hole. Tie a large knot at the end to keep the cord from coming back through. The knot should be on the inside of the lid.

5 Screw on the lid, leaving the free end of the cord sticking out.

YOU NEED

1-gallon plastic milk jug with lid

Sink

Towel

Scissors

Hammer

Large nail

Nylon or cotton cord about 46 cm (18 inches) long, the rougher the better

6   Hold the jug by the handle with one hand, and with your other hand, hold the cord between your thumb and forefinger.

7   Press your thumbnail snugly against the cord. Now abruptly pull down, rubbing your thumbnail against the cord. (Figure 8-1)

Figure 8-1

Q: What do you call a field of noisy dogs?
A: A barking lot!

8   Pull down two or three times in rapid succession. What type of
    sound do you hear?

WHAT HAPPENED?

Members of the dog family, which includes domestic (or pet) dogs,
as well as wild dogs such as wolves, coyotes, jackals, foxes, and
dingoes, make sounds with their vocal chords the same way we do.
Barks, growls, howls, yelps, and whimpers each communicate a
different message such as greeting, submission, play, and aggression.

Which kind of dog sound did your experiment most closely resemble?
If you have a dog, try the instrument on your dog to see how he
reacts. Does your dog bark back, or does he just look at you like
you've gone nuts?

Do all animals have vocal chords? Do you think that all animals
communicate with each other by making sounds?

CHECK THIS OUT

An important debate among scientists is whether animals automatically
know certain behaviors by instinct or are taught them by adults of
their species. This is called *nature versus nurture*. For example, doves
make the same cooing sounds no matter how they are raised. But
experiment suggests that birds with more complicated songs are
taught what song to sing. If a white crowned sparrow chick grows
up around a lot of different kinds of birds, it still is able to learn the
song its species is supposed to sing. If the chick is isolated from other
birds during its early life, it learns only a little of the song. If the
baby bird is deaf at an early age, its song is completely different
from the normal song.

Guess What?

★ Chimpanzees are one of the noisiest jungle animals. They scream, drum on trees, slap the ground, and are constantly hooting or muttering.

★ Dogs can hear a whistle producing 30,000 hertz. (Remember that humans can only hear sounds 20,000 hertz or less.) (Figure 8-2)

Figure 8-2

Don't be a dumbbell. This one's fun!

Clear as a Bell

Your Challenge

To produce and compare bell sounds from a funnel.

Do This

1 Tie a metal object to the end of one of the strings.

2 Thread the free end of the string through the large opening in the funnel, and drape the string on the outside of the small end.

3 Suspend the metal object inside the funnel, like the clapper of a bell, and give the funnel a shake. Notice the tone of the sound. Remove the metal object and string. (Figure 9-1)

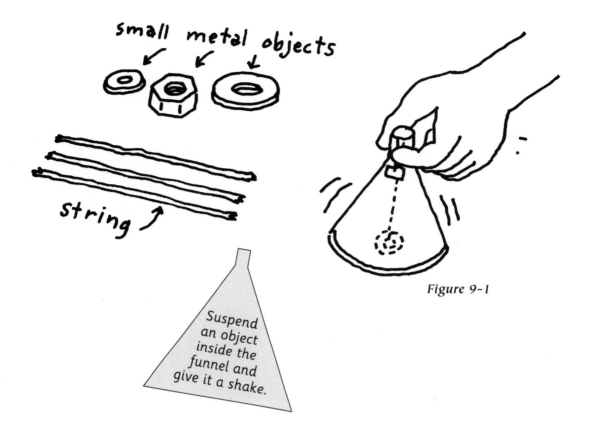

small metal objects

string →

Suspend an object inside the funnel and give it a shake.

Figure 9-1

4   Tie a different-sized object to another string and repeat the step. Now what tone do you hear? Remove this object. (Figure 9-2)

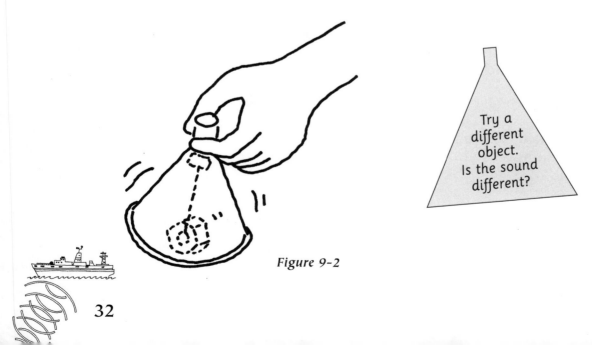

Try a different object. Is the sound different?

Figure 9-2

5 Tie the remaining object to the other string and repeat the step. How does this sound compare with the other two?

What Happened?

The sound you hear is the natural tone of the funnel. The only way you can change the tone is to change the size or shape of the funnel. The size of the clapper won't affect it.

Check This Out

Bells have been used since ancient times to get people's attention. They have announced the hour of day, sent soldiers to battle, and sounded fire alarms. The oldest bell, found near the ancient ruins of Babylon in present-day Iraq, is said to be more than 3,000 years old. The largest bell ever cast is the Czar Kolokol in Moscow. It weighs 181 metric tons (200 tons), is 6.5 meters in diameter (21 feet), and stands 6 meters high (19 feet). The bell was cracked in a fire in 1737 and has never been rung. By comparison, the bell in Big Ben in London is 2.3 meters high (7.5 feet) and weighs 12.2 metric tons (13.5 tons). (Figure 9-3)

Big Ben in London, England, refers to the bell and to the clock tower.

Figure 9-3

33

GUESS WHAT?

★ Before printing was developed, information sent to large groups of people was transmitted by drums, church bells, cannons, and horns.

★ A full symphony orchestra may have as many as 100 musicians to produce music. Some composers might include unusual sounds such as those made by a car horn, typewriter, and siren.

Have you ever wondered how music is produced from a record or compact disc? You won't after you do this one!

IT'S THE PITS!

YOUR CHALLENGE

To discover how sound is produced from the surface of an object.

DO THIS

1 Make a cone out of the paper and fasten it with tape.

2 Fold the small tip of the cone over. Carefully press the needle through the folded part, or have an adult do it.

3 Hold the large end of the needle (the end with the eye), and carefully touch the sharp end to one of the grooves in the file.

4 Slowly and with a light touch, move the point of the needle down the groove. What do you hear? (Figure 10-1)

YOU NEED

Sheet of paper about 22 × 28 cm (8.5 × 11 inches)

Transparent tape

Steel sewing needle

Metal file with grooves

Smooth surface, table top, desk top, etc.

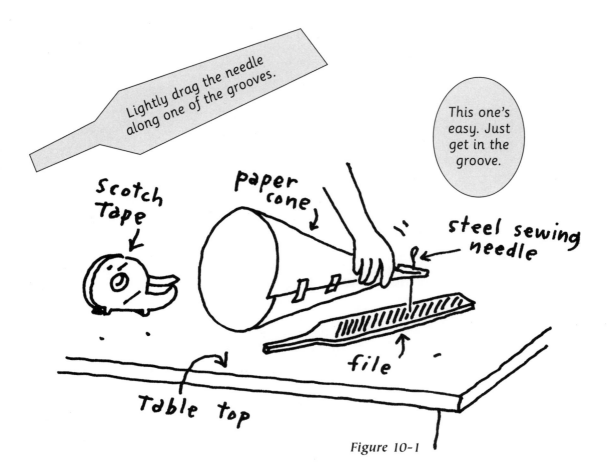

Lightly drag the needle along one of the grooves.

This one's easy. Just get in the groove.

Scotch Tape

paper cone

steel sewing needle

file

Table top

Figure 10-1

5 Touch the point of the needle to a desk or table and slowly drag the point over the surface. Now what do you hear? (Figure 10-2)

WHAT HAPPENED?

Phonograph records originally are smooth. When sound is recorded, tiny grooves are cut into the master disc. The grooves are cut at the same rate of vibration, or frequency, as the sound being recorded. When played back, the groove in the record causes the needle to vibrate at that same frequency and reproduces the original sound.

Unlike records, sounds are recorded on compact discs (CDs) by a *laser*, which is a device that produces a narrow, intense beam of light. Operating at the frequency of the original sound, the laser burns tiny oval pits in the surface. This leaves a thin spiral of pits and flat spaces, much like the grooves in a phonograph record. Because the pits are very

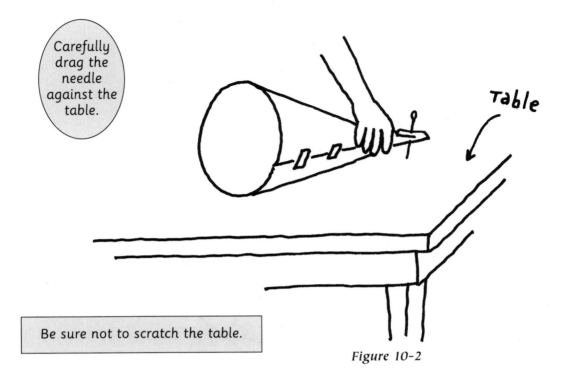

Carefully drag the needle against the table.

Table

Be sure not to scratch the table.

Figure 10-2

tiny and are spaced so close together, much more information can be stored on a CD than on a phonograph record. The file in your experiment has grooves like a record, while the desk surface is made up of tiny pits like a CD.

When sound is recorded on tape, the tape is coated with a chemical called *iron oxide*. The iron oxide particles normally are in a random pattern. The recording process magnetizes these particles, causing them to form a regular pattern. When the tape is played, the magnetized particles produce electrical signals. These signals are then sent to a speaker, which changes the signals into sound.

CHECK THIS OUT

Do you know what the difference is between FM and AM radio? FM stands for *frequency modulation*; AM stands for *amplitude modulation*. FM technology has a greater freedom from interference caused by thunderstorms and electrical systems in cars. This is why FM stations often sound clearer than AM stations.

GUESS WHAT?

★ The groove on a record begins on the outer edge and spirals toward the hole in the center. Compact discs, on the other hand, are read beginning at the center and spiral outward.

★ Compact discs are able to reproduce such high-quality sounds because when a recording is made, the electronic circuits read the original sounds about 40,000 times each second.

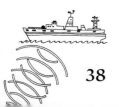

Play a song on drinking glasses!

WHAT'S THE HITCH WITH PITCH?

YOUR CHALLENGE

To make musical sounds by changing pitch.

DO THIS

1   Arrange the glasses in a row and fill the first one nearly to the top with water. Tap it with the pencil and notice the sound.

2   Fill the second glass with water, but not as full as the first. Tap it with the pencil. How does this sound compare with the sound from the first glass?

3   Adjust the water level of the second glass to make the next-highest note from the first glass. Was the water level raised or lowered?

YOU NEED

Eight tall drinking glasses

Water

Pencil

4   Repeat the steps with the remaining glasses, with each glass having a little less water. It will take some experimenting to find the proper water levels, but when you have them tuned, you will be able to make musical sounds. (Figure 11-1)

Tap the glasses with a pencil.

water

Figure 11-1

WHAT HAPPENED?

The tapping pencil causes the glass to vibrate and produce the sound. The water *dampens*, or slows, these vibrations. So, the less water in the glass, the faster the glass vibrates and the higher the pitch.

Try to play an entire song on the glasses. You might need to adjust the water levels more to get the notes you need.

CHECK THIS OUT

Look around the house for other things that might make good musical instruments. For instance, use walnut shells or bottle caps to make castanets, pot lids to make cymbals, a soda pop bottle to make a flute, or wooden dowels to make rhythm sticks. (Figure 11-2)

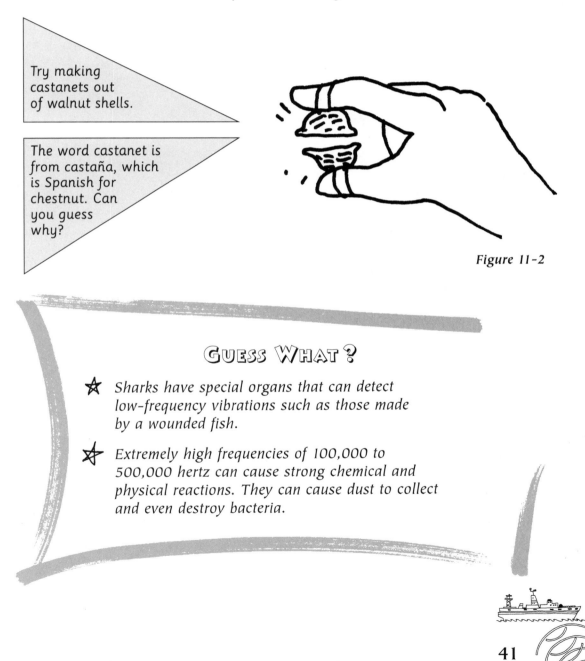

Try making castanets out of walnut shells.

The word castanet is from castaña, which is Spanish for chestnut. Can you guess why?

Figure 11-2

GUESS WHAT?

☆ Sharks have special organs that can detect low-frequency vibrations such as those made by a wounded fish.

☆ Extremely high frequencies of 100,000 to 500,000 hertz can cause strong chemical and physical reactions. They can cause dust to collect and even destroy bacteria.

Make a soda-bottle flute to understand pitch.

PITCH SWITCHER

YOUR CHALLENGE

To observe different pitches from the same source.

DO THIS

1 Pour a small amount of water into one of the bottles. Fill the second bottle with a little more water than the first.

2 Fill the third bottle with more water than the second bottle.

3 Fill the fourth bottle with more water than the third bottle. It should be almost full.

4 Blow across the top of the first bottle, resting your chin against the bottle. Aim the stream of air so that it hits just inside the edge on the other side of the opening. Listen to the sound. (Figure 12-1)

Water

Four empty glass bottles, the same size

Pencil

Figure 12-1

5 Blow across the second, third, and fourth bottles. What happens to the pitch?

6 Now, tap the first bottle with the pencil. Listen to the sound.

7 Tap the second, third, and fourth bottles. What happened to the pitch this time? (Figure 12-2)

WHAT HAPPENED?

When you blew across the top of the bottle, a wave of compressed air traveled down the inside of the bottle. It struck the surface of the water and was reflected back up toward the opening. When the compressed air left the opening, the air expanded, sending another wave down toward the bottom of the bottle. The compressed and expanded waves travel up and down the inside of the bottle, passing right through each other.

Figure 12-2

When these waves reach the opening of the bottle, they force the stream of air from your lips to swing back and forth across the opening. The stream of air is vibrating. When this vibrating stream strikes the surrounding air, it produces the sound.

The waves travel farther inside the bottle with the least amount of water. This causes the air to vibrate slower. The more water in the bottle, the shorter the distance the air travels. This makes the waves return very quickly and makes the stream of air vibrate faster.

When you tapped the bottles with the pencil, the sound was produced by the vibrating glass. The water slowed, or dampened, the vibrations. So the more water in the bottle, the slower the glass vibrated.

Can you think of a musical instrument that is played by blowing air across an opening, like you did with the bottle?

CHECK THIS OUT

Listen to your favorite piece of music. Now that you know what pitch is, note how the pitch changes. Also notice the loudness, or *volume*. Do some parts of the song sound louder than others?

GUESS WHAT ?

⭐ *Elephants and some whales communicate at a frequency too low for humans to hear. (Figure 12-3)*

⭐ *Kettledrums are made with a hole in the bottom to relieve the stress of the vibrations created by the sound waves.*

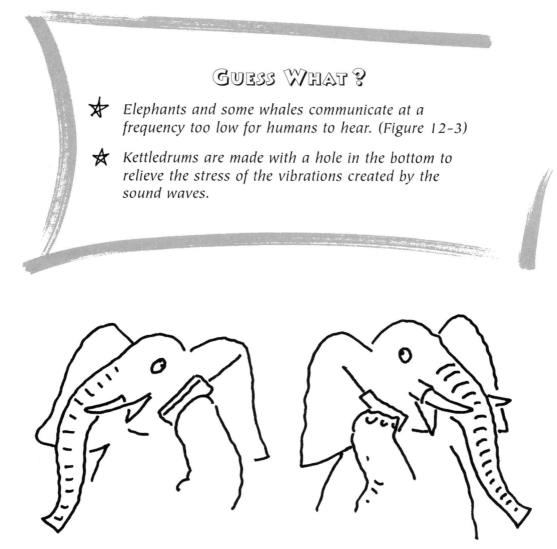

Figure 12-3

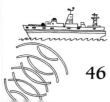

You'll get good vibes from this experiment.

RESONATE WITH A FRIEND

YOUR CHALLENGE

To observe the natural vibration rate of two objects.

DO THIS

1   Hold the mouth of one of the bottles near your ear.

2   Ask your partner to stand about 1 meter (3 feet) to one side of you and blow across the top of the other bottle until a clear note is produced. How does the bottle you're holding respond? (Figure 13-1)

Figure 13-1

WHAT HAPPENED?

All objects have a natural rate of vibration depending on their size and shape. When two objects have the same natural rate of vibration, one can make the other one vibrate. If two guitars are tuned the same, a string set to vibrating on one will cause the same string to vibrate on the other. The two instruments are said to be in *resonance*.

CHECK THIS OUT

Acoustics are the study of how sound waves behave and how they can be controlled. Acoustical engineers design auditoriums with a combination of sound-absorbing and sound-reflecting materials. In this manner, they can control echo and reverberation. Many auditoriums are also designed so that voices can be heard from the stage to the back of the room without artificial amplification. When you are at school, notice how the shape of the room affects sound. For instance, a long hallway with the walls close together and with uncovered walls and floors have a greater tendency to produce echoes. Rooms with carpeting and wall coverings muffle sound.

Guess What?

- *Members of the cat family are the only animals that purr. The animal vibrates its vocal cords in a continuous hum.*
- *A pet turtle probably can't hear you talk to it. They are only sensitive to sound waves of about 100 hertz. The sound waves that produce human speech range from about 250 to 6,000 hertz. (Figure 13-2)*

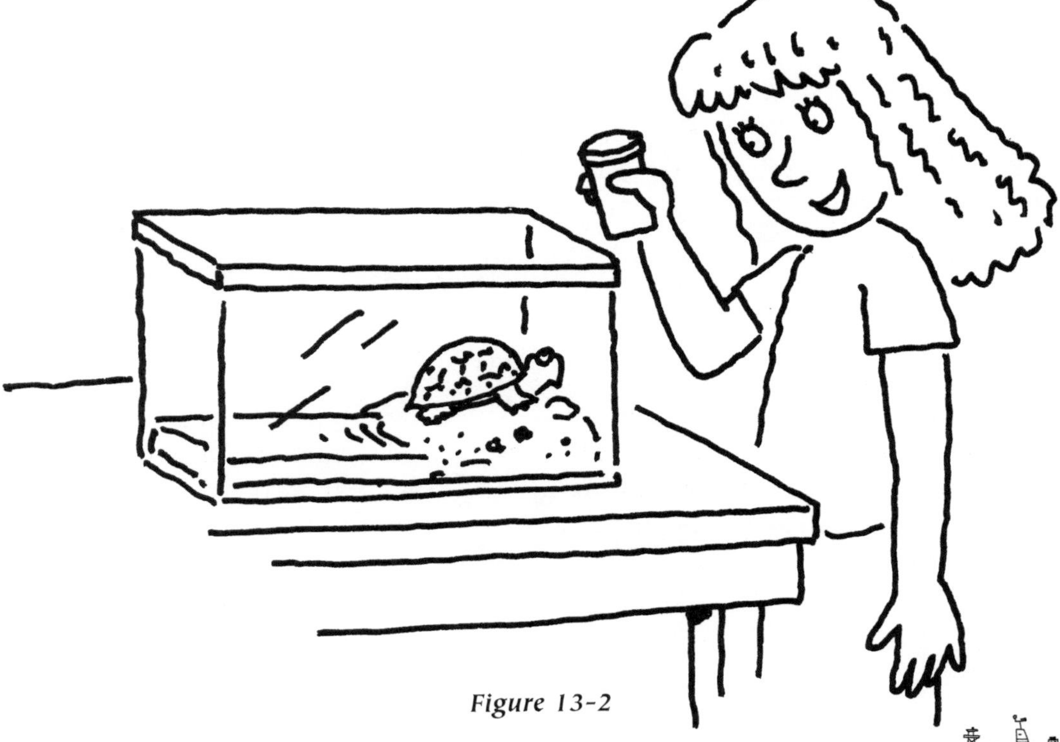

Figure 13-2

Hang out with this experiment
to see how weights relate.

LET'S SWING!

YOUR CHALLENGE

To observe resonance between suspended objects.

DO THIS

1 Tie one of the strings between the two supports, making sure the string is taut.

2 Tie the remaining three strings at equal spaces along the support string.

3 Tie a weight to each of the three strings, making sure each weight is at a different height on each string. Tie the knot so that it can easily be undone.

4 Allow the weights to settle down, then set one to swing from side to side like a pendulum. What do the other weights do?

5 Swing each of the weights in turn. What do you observe?

YOU NEED

Four pieces of string at least 1 meter (3 feet) long

Two upright supports; for instance, two table legs, two chairs, etc.

Three identical weights the same size; for instance, three nuts or three bolts

6 Untie two of the weights and suspend them at the same height as each other, but at a different height than the third weight. Swing one of these weights. What happens to the other two? (Figure 14-1)

Suspend two of the weights at the same height.

Figure 14-1

7 Suspend all three weights at the same height and repeat the steps. Now what do you observe? (Figure 14-2)

Suspend all three weights at the same height.

Figure 14-2

52

WHAT HAPPENED?

When one pendulum is set in motion, it has a natural frequency. If any other pendulum is at the same length, it will have the same natural frequency as the one in motion. If all three are suspended at the same length, they will all have the same natural frequency. When one pendulum is set in motion, another will feel the tiny vibrations traveling down the string and start to swing because it will have the same natural frequency as the first pendulum. These vibrations are called *sympathetic vibrations.*

Resonance occurs when small vibrations of one object at its natural frequency produce large vibrations in another object with the same natural frequency. The small vibrations are the sympathetic vibrations from the first pendulum, which set the other pendulums in motion.

CHECK THIS OUT

Have you ever heard of an opera singer being able to break a crystal glass by singing a certain note? This happens because the singer is singing a note at the natural frequency of the glass. In other words, if the singer *precisely* reproduces the note that is heard from the glass when it is tapped, the glass will shatter. (Figure 14-3)

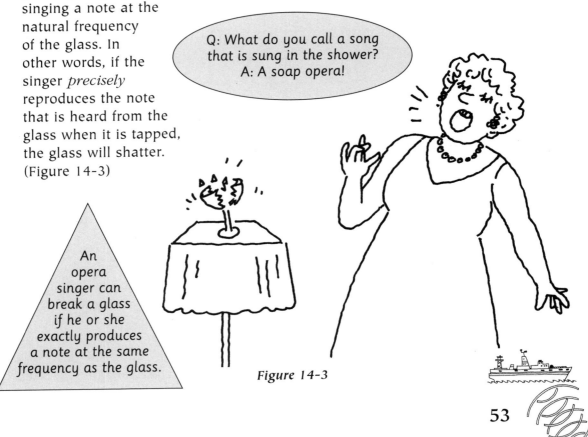

Q: What do you call a song that is sung in the shower?
A: A soap opera!

An opera singer can break a glass if he or she exactly produces a note at the same frequency as the glass.

Figure 14-3

GUESS WHAT?

✰ Soldiers marching in step across a bridge can create sympathetic vibrations strong enough to cause the bridge to collapse. For this reason, they always march out of step when crossing bridges.

✰ In the deep oceans there are places where sounds travel great distances called sound channels. For example, if a small explosion was set off in the sound channel near San Francisco, California, the sound can be detected 4,023 kilometers (2,500 miles) away by an instrument called a hydrophone that is suspended in the sound channel near the Hawaiian islands.

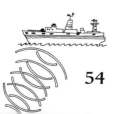

Did you know glass can sing? Here's how!

FRICTION ADDICTION

YOUR CHALLENGE

To produce a sound from friction.

DO THIS

1 Pour a little water into the glass. Add a few drops of vinegar.

2 Dip one of your fingers into the water and slowly rub it around the rim of the glass. Use a smooth, steady motion. What do you hear? (Figure 15-1)

WHAT HAPPENED?

The vinegar is used to remove the oil from your fingertip and the rim of the glass. Your finger produces vibrations in the glass the same way a violin bow produces vibrations in the strings of a violin.

YOU NEED

Water

Drinking glass with thin walls

Vinegar

Rub a moistened finger along the rim.

thin drinking glass

VINEGAR

water and vinegar

Figure 15-1

You might need to dip your finger back in the water a few times.

What do you think would happen if you used different sizes of glasses and different amounts of water. Try it and see!

CHECK THIS OUT

The instrument you made in this experiment resembles an instrument called the glass harmonica. This instrument was invented by Ben Franklin in the 1760s. Unlike the mouth-organ type of harmonica, the glass harmonica consisted of a set of bowls of various sizes filled with different amounts of water. These bowls rotated on a spindle that was attached to a pedal. A trough of water kept the bowls continually wet. The musician would play the instrument by rubbing his or her fingers along the wet edges of the bowls, just as you did. Composers such as Mozart and Beethoven even wrote pieces for the glass harmonica.

GUESS WHAT?

★ Ultrasonics, or ultrasounds, *are the sound levels above the range of human hearing. They can be used to observe the movement of an unborn child, to detect flaws in metals, and to detect underwater signaling called* sonar.

★ Bats can hear and produce ultrasounds up to 100,000 hertz.

★ *During a drought, when trees do not get enough water, they also make ultrasonic sounds. These are too high pitched to be heard by humans, but they can be detected by special instruments. (Figure 15-2)*

Figure 15-2

Try this tubular experiment!

SOUND SCRUNCHING

YOUR CHALLENGE

To discover what happens when sound waves are kept from spreading out.

DO THIS

1   Hold the clock near your ear and notice the ticking sound. (Figure 16-1)

Listen to the sound of the clock near your ear.

Figure 16-1

2   Slowly move the clock away until you no longer hear it. How far
    can you hear the clock ticking?

3   Place the cardboard tube against your ear
    and hold the clock near
    the open end.
    Now what
    do you hear?
    (Figure 16-2)

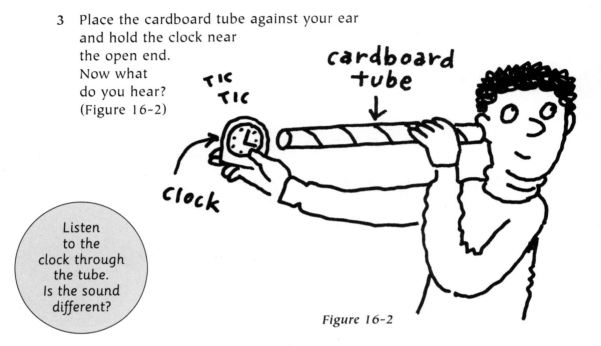

TIC
TIC

cardboard
tube

clock

Listen
to the
clock through
the tube.
Is the sound
different?

Figure 16-2

WHAT HAPPENED?

Sound needs energy to travel. When sound spreads outward from its
source, it travels in waves in all directions, losing energy as it goes until
no sound is heard. When sound waves are funneled in a single direction,
less energy is lost and the sound travels farther.

Could this help explain the shape of the bell on horn instruments?

CHECK THIS OUT

Make a list of all the musical instruments you can think of where sound
is made by blowing air into them. Draw the instruments, or think about
the shape of each one. How do you think their shapes affect the sounds
they produce?

Guess What?

★ Recording studios use multitrack recorders. These recorders use up to 48 different tracks, or narrow strips in the recording tape, that can be recorded separately. This means, for example, that a guitarist could record at one time and a singer could record a day or so later. The volume, or loudness, of one track does not affect the volume of the other tracks. This allows a sound engineer to alter the sounds and volumes, called mixing, to create a totally new recording.

★ Sir Isaac Newton used the echo of a hallway at Trinity College to measure the speed of sound. He stamped his foot at one end of the hall and measured the time it took for the sound to bounce off the far wall and return as an echo. Since he knew the distance to the far wall, he was able to calculate the speed at which sound travels. In fact, his speed of sound was within a few feet per second of the current speed accepted by today's scientists.

Make this low-tech telephone
to talk to a friend!

GARDEN HOSE TELEPHONE

YOUR CHALLENGE

To use a garden hose to communicate.

DO THIS

1 Stretch the hose out to its full length. Blow hard through one end to make sure the hose is empty of water.

2 Now ask your partner to speak in one end while you listen in the other end. What do you hear? (Figure 17-1)

Figure 17-1

WHAT HAPPENED?

Trapping the sound waves in the hose concentrates the vibrations, allowing the sound to travel farther than in the outside air. You will have to take turns talking and listening, but you will be able to hear each other clearly. As long as you don't put any kinks in the hose, you can still hear even when you bend the hose around a corner. In the past, a similar method was used to send orders from the bridge of a ship to the engine room.

Do you think this is the same reason a megaphone makes the voice of someone speaking into it louder?

CHECK THIS OUT

Ever wonder why people cup their hands around their mouths when they're calling to someone far away? They're concentrating the sound waves by making a kind of megaphone with their hands. Try amplifying your voice by holding your hands around your mouth in various positions. Which position works best?

GUESS WHAT?

☆ *In Africa, drums called "talking drums" are used to communicate over many miles. These unique drums can reproduce the tones and rhythms of the local language.*

☆ *The people of the Canary Islands use "whistle talk" to communicate over long distances. These whistles represent words of their spoken language.*

Did you know sound can bounce?
This experiment will show you!

BOUNCING SOUND

YOUR CHALLENGE

To hear a reflected sound.

DO THIS

1 With one hand, hold the watch or clock above the table. With the other hand, place one end of the tube near the clock, and angle the tube downward so the other end is near the top of the table.

2 Ask someone to hold the other tube at an opposite angle, so the tubes make a "V," and listen at the end of their tube. Your partner should plug the other ear with his or her finger to reduce outside sounds. (Figure 18-1)

Ticking watch or clock

Two empty paper-towel cardboard tubes

Table

A partner

Ask your friend to listen at the end of the other tube.

TICK TOCK

Figure 18-1

3 When the positions of the tubes are just right, the ticking can be heard coming out of the end of the second tube.

WHAT HAPPENED?

The sound waves travel down the first tube and are reflected off the surface of the table into the second tube. They then travel up the second tube and are heard at the opening. Sound waves can be reflected much like rays of light are reflected by a mirror. (Figure 18-2)

Sound waves bounce off surfaces in much the same way that a light beam reflects off a mirror.

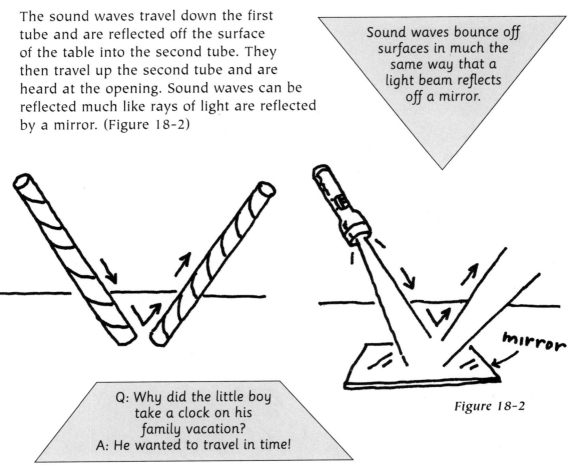

Q: Why did the little boy take a clock on his family vacation?
A: He wanted to travel in time!

Figure 18-2

Do the tubes need to be angled at a "V" to work? Try it again, but this time have your partner angle the tube lower or higher than your tube. What happens? What does this tell you about sound waves?

How do you think knowing about the behavior of sound waves can help in the design of a concert hall?

CHECK THIS OUT

An echo occurs when sound waves bounce off a solid object. The farther you are from the object you shout toward, the longer the delay between your shout and the resulting echo. Test this out the next time you hear an echo.

GUESS WHAT?

⭐ *Honeybees use wing vibrations to produce sounds that tell other bees the exact distance from the hive to a source of nectar. (Figure 18-3)*

⭐ *Some insects detect sound waves with their antennas, while katydids and crickets use sensitive hairs on their front legs.*

Figure 18-3

Find out what shock waves are.

WAVE RAVE

YOUR CHALLENGE

To produce and observe the effects of a shock wave.

DO THIS

1 Tape one end of the bathroom tissue to the edge of a table, arm of a chair, or some other support so that the free end hangs down in an open space.

2 Ask an adult to help you cut off the bottom of the plastic bottle with the scissors.

3 Fold the plastic wrap in half *twice* to make it stronger. Smooth the plastic into a flat layer, or use the piece of balloon.

4 Stretch the plastic or balloon piece over the open bottom of the bottle and fasten it in place with the rubber band. (Figure 19-1)

YOU NEED

Support, such as the edge of a table or a chair arm

Tape

Sheet of bathroom tissue about 46 cm (18 inches) long

Scissors

Clean, 12-ounce plastic soda bottle

Sheet of plastic food wrap about 50 cm (20 inches) long or a piece of a balloon large enough to stretch over bottom of bottle

Rubber band

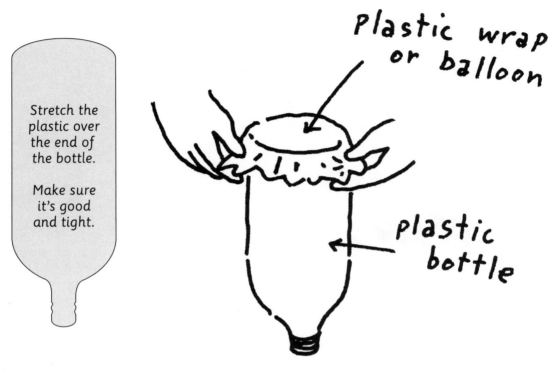

Plastic wrap or balloon

plastic bottle

Figure 19-1

5   Hold the bottle about 1 meter (3 feet) from the tissue paper. Aim the small end of the bottle at the bathroom tissue and thump the plastic with your finger. What happens to the tissue? (Figure 19-2)

6   Hold the bottle farther away and thump the plastic again. How far from the paper can you hold the bottle and still produce the effect? Does the tissue move the instant you thump the plastic? What sound do you hear?

WHAT HAPPENED?

Shock waves are caused by the sudden compression, or squeezing together, of the surrounding air. These shock waves have been known to travel great distances. The shock wave you created was strong enough

Figure 19-2

to jolt the tissue paper, but was at too low of a frequency to be heard as sound. The only sound you heard was that caused by the thump. The human ear can detect sound vibrations of about 20 to 20,000 hertz.

Check This Out

When a meteor, or shooting star, enters the earth's atmosphere, it is traveling at speeds of 1,800 to 8,400 kilometers an hour (1,100 to 5,200 miles an hour). Since this is faster than the surrounding air, shock waves are created. These shock waves cause a sonic boom. The heat from the friction of the meteor's journey is so intense that the surface of the meteor reaches the boiling point and melts away. Most meteors turn to dust before they reach the earth. In fact, millions of these burned-out meteors fall to the earth every day.

Guess What?

★ *Fin whales have a joint at the tip of their lower jaw that they pop like a huge knuckle while feeding. This produces powerful pulses or vibrations, starting at the front of the jaw and reverberating back along the sides. The shock waves caused by these vibrations keep the startled prey in the middle of the whale's mouth, preventing it from escaping.*

★ *When the volcano Krakatoa erupted in Indonesia on an afternoon in 1883, the explosion was heard the next morning 3,540 kilometers (2,200 miles) away in Australia. (Figure 19-3)*

Figure 19-3

Try this experiment to learn which sounds can turn a corner.

SOUND SHADOWS

YOUR CHALLENGE

To discover why some sound waves bend.

DO THIS

1   Place the clock or timer on the table and stand about 1.5 meters (5 feet) away. Face the clock and listen to the ticking.

2   Plug one ear with your finger. What do you hear?

3   Still listening closely, slowly turn to the side so that your open ear is facing directly away from the clock. Now what do you hear? (Figure 20-1)

YOU NEED

Ticking clock or kitchen timer

Table

Figure 20-1

What Happened?

The ticking of the clock is a high-pitched sound. High-pitched sounds are made up mostly of short waves, and short waves don't bend much. When you stood facing the clock, the short sound waves were able to enter your ear. However, when you turned to the side, with the plugged ear facing the clock, your head blocked off the sound waves. In effect, your head made a "shadow" where most of the short waves were unable to travel. Low-pitched sounds are the results of longer waves that can bend easily.

When you hear a marching band, you can hear the music from around a corner. Most of the sounds you hear, however, are from low-pitched instruments like the drums and trombones. The longer waves will bend around corners. Higher-pitched instruments like the flute will not be heard until you can see them because they produce shorter waves that don't bend easily.

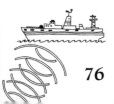

CHECK THIS OUT

Next time you hear a marching band in the distance, try to pick out which instruments you are hearing.

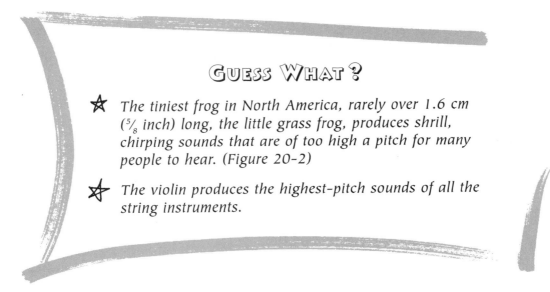

GUESS WHAT?

★ *The tiniest frog in North America, rarely over 1.6 cm (⅝ inch) long, the little grass frog, produces shrill, chirping sounds that are of too high a pitch for many people to hear. (Figure 20-2)*

★ *The violin produces the highest-pitch sounds of all the string instruments.*

Figure 20-2

Find out what happens when sound waves
are stretched, squished, and scrunched.

TRAIN DRAIN

YOUR CHALLENGE

To hear the effects of squeezing and stretching sound waves.

DO THIS

1 Listen to the sound of a train or an emergency vehicle.
   What do you hear as it approaches? (Figure 21-1)

2 Listen as it goes by. What happens to the pitch of
   the sound?

3 Now listen to the sound as the vehicle moves away. What
   pitch do you hear now?

Listen to
the train as it
approaches.
How does the sound change?

Figure 21-1

WHAT HAPPENED?

As the source of the sound approaches, the sound waves are pushed closer together. More sound waves strike your ear each second. This means the frequency of the sound waves is higher. Since the frequency is higher, the pitch seems higher. When the source of the sound passes and starts moving away, the sound waves are stretched apart. Fewer sound waves strike your ear each second, so the frequency is lower. Because the frequency is lower, the pitch will sound lower. The sound actually has only one pitch.

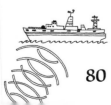

This apparent change in pitch is called the *Doppler effect* after the German physicist Christian Doppler, who described the principle in 1842. The Doppler effect is the apparent change in frequency of sound, light, or radio waves caused by motion.

CHECK THIS OUT

You can notice the Doppler effect in many different sounds. For example, listen to how the noise from a car changes as it passes on the highway or when going around a track in a car race. You could also have a friend ride by on a bike, skateboard, or skates while blowing a whistle to see how the sound is affected. (Figure 21-2)

Listen to the sound of a car as it drives past.

Q: When is a car not a car? A: When it turns into a driveway!

Figure 21-2

GUESS WHAT?

★ Crickets and spiders have membranes that are something like sounding boards on their legs.

★ Moths have a type of ear that uses membranes much like a sounding board to warn them when bats are near.

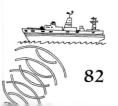

How does water affect sound?
Try this experiment and see.

SOUNDS WITHOUT BOUNDS

YOUR CHALLENGE

To discover how different materials affect the speed of sound.

DO THIS

1   Place your ear against the surface of one end of the table and ask your partner to tap the other end with the point of a pencil. What do you hear? (Figure 22-1)

2   Now, fill the bucket about three-fourths full of water and place your ear against the side.

3   Ask your partner to lower the comb about halfway down into the water and rub his or her fingernail across the teeth. What sounds do you hear? (Figure 22-2)

YOU NEED

Wooden table

Pencil

Metal bucket

Water

Comb

A partner

With your ear against the table,
listen to the tapping sound.

Figure 22-1

WHAT HAPPENED?

Normally, we hear sounds brought to us through vibrations in the air, but sound can travel very well through wood, water, even your teeth and the bones in your head.

CHECK THIS OUT

Using a tape recorder, record yourself reading a paragraph from this book. Play the tape back. Does your voice sound different to you? Can you guess why? Now record a friend's voice. Does your friend think his or her voice sounds different? Does it sound different to you?

Have your partner thumb the comb in the water as you listen.

Figure 22-2

GUESS WHAT?

⭐ The speed of sound in ordinary water is about 1,498 meters (4,915 feet) per second, but because of the density of seawater, it increases to 1,531 meters (5,223 feet) per second.

⭐ The speed of sound in aluminum is about 5,100 meters (16,700 feet) per second.

Crank up the volume for this one!

BAKING PAN AMP

YOUR CHALLENGE

To discover how vibrations can be amplified.

DO THIS

1 Tie one end of the string to the handle of one of the forks. Tie the other end of the string through the hole in the end of the pan.

2 Place the pan upside down on a table or countertop. The end with the string should be sticking out over the edge so that the fork is suspended below.

3 Lift the fork by the string and tap it with the other fork. Notice the sound. (Figure 23-1)

YOU NEED

String about 60 cm (2 feet) long

Two forks

Metal baking pan with hole on lip of one end

Hold the fork up by the string and tap it with the other fork.

Heavy baking pan

Table

2' string

metal forks

Figure 23-1

4   Release the string so that the fork hangs freely from the pan. Tap the fork again. Now what happens to the sound? (Figure 23-2)

Tap the fork as it hangs from the pan.

Figure 23-2

WHAT HAPPENED?

The first sound was made by the vibrations of the fork alone. The second sound was also made by vibrations from the fork, but the string carried the vibrations to the pan. Because the pan is larger than the fork, it vibrated a larger amount of air. This caused the sound to be *amplified*, or become louder.

CHECK THIS OUT

Have you ever heard of a tuning fork? A *tuning fork* is used as a standard to tune instruments. Tuning forks are usually set to an "A" pitch, and vibrate at 440 vibrations per second. Ask your teacher if he or she has a tuning fork. Then, strike the tuning fork and dip it in a glass of water. You'll see waves caused by the vibrations. (Figure 23-3)

You can observe waves caused by the tuning fork as it vibrates.

You can tune a fork, but can you tunafish?

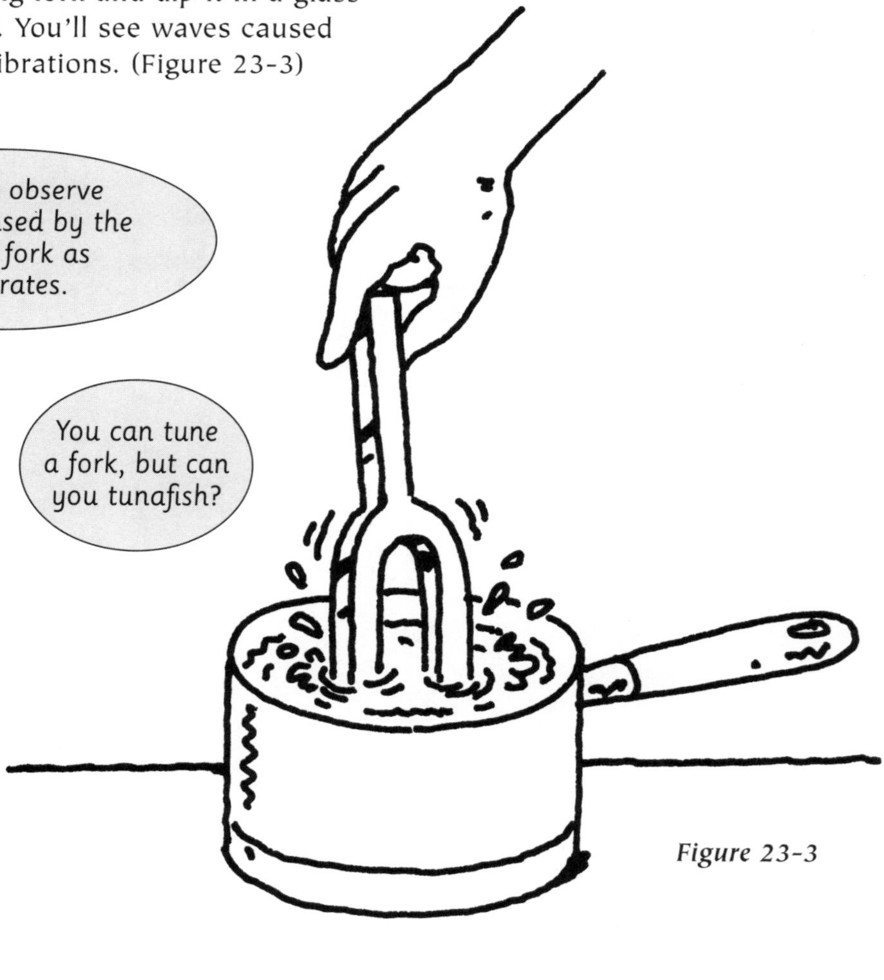

Figure 23-3

GUESS WHAT?

⭐ Because snakes do not have external ear openings, eardrums, and middle-ear cavities, they cannot detect most airborne sounds. A rattlesnake doesn't even hear its own rattle. They can, however, easily detect ground vibrations through the bone in their jaw and skull.

⭐ The famous architect Frank Lloyd Wright designed a home where the living room and terrace is suspended over a small waterfall. Although the home is beautiful, it was unoccupied most of the time because of the noise from the waterfall. Today it is a museum.

Make a simple amplifier
with a drinking glass.

TURN UP
THE VOLUME!

YOUR CHALLENGE

To amplify sound (in other words, make it louder) through different substances.

DO THIS

⚠ 1 Place the glass near the edge of the table and hold your ear a few inches above the opening.

2 With your ear still to the glass, grip the handle of the fork firmly and tap the other end with the handle of the knife. It might take two or three tries, but you can make the fork ring.

3 When the fork rings, touch the handle to the table about 60 cm (2 feet) from the glass. What do you hear? (Figure 24-1)

YOU NEED

Drinking glass with thin walls

Wooden table

Fork

Butter or table knife

Touch the handle of the fork to the table.

Figure 24-1

WHAT HAPPENED?

When the fork was first struck, you hear the sound only faintly. The sound traveled directly to your ear through vibrations in the air. When you touched the fork to the table, the vibrations traveled through the wood to the glass, where the sound was amplified.

CHECK THIS OUT

If you have a phone where the handset unscrews, try unscrewing the mouthpiece (make sure to ask an adult first). Inside, you'll find a disk with holes in it. This is a simple amplifier called a carbon microphone. Microphones amplify sounds by changing the energy of the sound into an electrical current.

GUESS WHAT?

★ The Corythosaurus, a dinosaur that lived 90 million years ago, had a hollow crest on its head, which may have been a resonating chamber to amplify sounds.

★ Mongolian ruler Genghis Khan used whistling arrows to direct his archers toward the enemy.

Use a screwdriver to hear sounds.

PIPE SCREAMS

YOUR CHALLENGE

To hear sounds transmitted through water pipes.

DO THIS

1   Make sure that no water is running in the house.

2   Now go to the outside faucet and place the tip of a screwdriver against the pipe near the faucet. Press your forehead against the top of the screwdriver. What do you hear? (Figure 25-1)

3   Ask your partner to turn on the cold water faucet at one of the sinks inside and let a small stream of water run.

4   Now use the screwdriver to listen to the outside faucet. What do you hear now? Ask your friend to turn off the water. Was there a change in the sound?

YOU NEED

Kitchen or bathroom sink

Outside faucet

Screwdriver

Piece of metal, such as a butter knife or spoon

A partner

This is a screwy way to hear!

Figure 25-1

5   Now ask the friend to use a piece of metal to tap out a signal on the pipe under the sink.

6   Place the screwdriver between your forehead and the outside faucet again. What do you hear? Do sounds travel through bone?

WHAT HAPPENED?

Vibrations travel much farther through water and metal compared to air.

Because sound travels so well through water, ships can use echo sounders to measure the depth of the water. These devices, located at the bottom of the ship, send out a series of sounds that are reflected off the bottom of the ocean floor. By measuring how long the sound takes to bounce off the ocean floor and return to the ship, they can tell how deep the ocean is at that point. Measurements done in this manner are called *soundings*. (Figure 25-2)

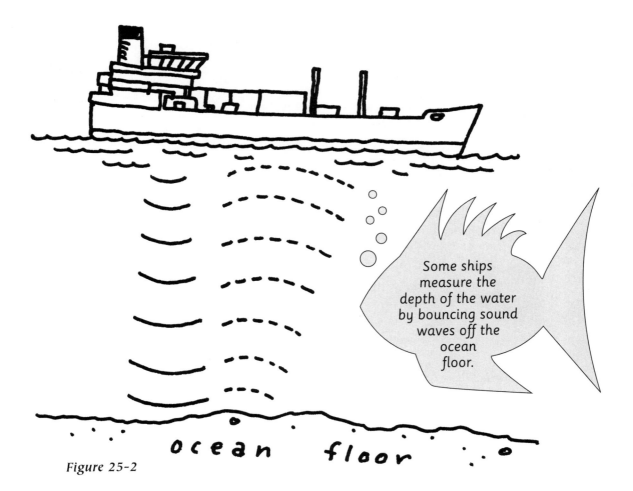

Some ships measure the depth of the water by bouncing sound waves off the ocean floor.

ocean floor

Figure 25-2

CHECK THIS OUT

Sea mammals such as whales and dolphins produce many different sounds. In fact, scientists today are studying whether they have an entire language of their own. Dolphins make clicking sounds to communicate.

The humpback whale makes the loudest sound of any creature on earth. Its call has been measured at 190 decibels, which is louder than a Concorde jet taking off!

GUESS WHAT?

★ Bats can produce and receive sounds of about 100,000 hertz, which they use for echolocation. *Echolocation* is a way to determine the location of an object by sending and then detecting sound waves that reflect from the object as an echo.

★ Geese honk continuously when migrating to let each other know where they are so they don't collide. (Figure 25-3)

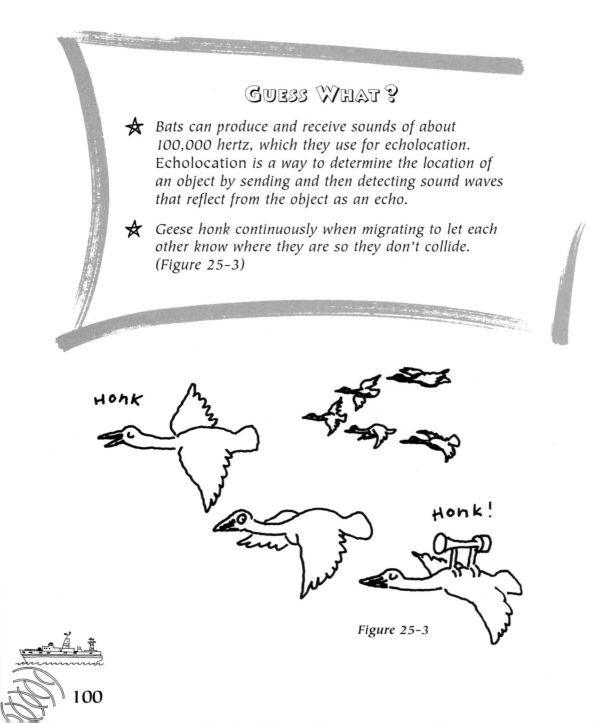

HONK

Honk!

Figure 25-3

Can you have sound without vibration?
You'll find out here!

KILL THAT NOISE!

YOUR CHALLENGE

To observe how reducing vibrations affects sound.

DO THIS

1 Tie one end of the string around the handle of the fork.

2 Hold the other end of the string in one hand and tap the prongs of the fork with the butter knife. What do you hear?

3 Wedge pieces of toothpicks or paper between the prongs of the fork.

4 Tap the fork again. Now what do you hear? (Figure 26-1)

YOU NEED

String

Fork

Butter knife

Toothpicks or small pieces of twisted paper

After wedging toothpicks or paper between the prongs, tap the fork with the knife.

Does it still ring?

Q: What do you call the sound churchbells make when people get married?
A: A wedding ring!

Figure 26-1

WHAT HAPPENED?

When the fork was first tapped, the prongs were free to vibrate and make sound waves. When the toothpicks were wedged in place, however, the vibrations were dampened and could not produce the ringing sound.

CHECK THIS OUT

Can you guess why the radio cuts off while you're in a car that drives under a bridge or into a tunnel? Here's a clue: Antennas are used to receive radio waves.

GUESS WHAT?

★ *Fish have no voice, but some do produce sounds. Croakers produce short two- and three-beat drum rolls, and ocean sunfish and hogfish grind their teeth to produce sounds. (Figure 26-2)*

★ *Some fish produce croaking, drumming, and grunting sounds from organs called* swim bladders.

Figure 26-2

This one will make your ears ring.

SPOON TUNES

YOUR CHALLENGE

To observe how our ears detect sound vibrations.

DO THIS

1   Tie small loops in each end of the string, and tie the middle of the string around the spoon.

2   Put a finger through each loop and then into each ear.

3   Lean over and let the suspended spoon gently bump the edge of a table or chair. What do you hear? (Figure 27-1)

4   Try it again with a fork or a butter knife. What happens to the tone of the sound?

5   Now use a thin copper wire instead of the string. Is the sound softer or louder? Why do you think it changed?

YOU NEED

String about 1 meter (3 feet) long

Metal spoon

Fork or butter knife

Thin copper wire about 1 meter (3 feet) long

Lean over so that the spoon bumps against the table.

Just don't let anyone see you doing this. You'll look pretty silly!

Figure 27-1

What Happened?

The vibrations from the spoon travel up the string to your eardrums. There, nerves transmit the sound waves to the brain, which changes them to sound. Because of the shape of the spoon—in other words, its curves and different thicknesses—a variety of sounds are produced. Some of these are produced by *overtones*, or partial tones. These are higher tones that are heard with the basic tones. Overtones vibrate at a frequency that is an exact multiple of the frequency of the basic tone.

Check This Out

Have you ever noticed that words beginning with an *sn-* sound often have to do with the nose? For instance, *sneeze* and *sniffle*. Even the word *snob* refers to someone with his or her nose in the air. See how many other words you can come up with that start with *sn-* and have something to do with the nose.

GUESS WHAT ?

★ Between childhood and adulthood, boys sometimes find their voices crack and are unable to hold the pitch. This is because their voice box is growing larger and the vocal cords have not yet adjusted to their size. (Figure 27-2)

★ Women usually have higher-pitched voices than men because a woman's vocal cords are shorter and thinner.

Figure 27-2

Talk to a friend with this simple telephone.

HOMEGROWN TELEPHONE

YOUR CHALLENGE

To construct and use a simple telephone.

DO THIS

1 Begin by waxing the string.
   Run the wax, back and
   forth, over the string
   several times. (Figure 28-1)

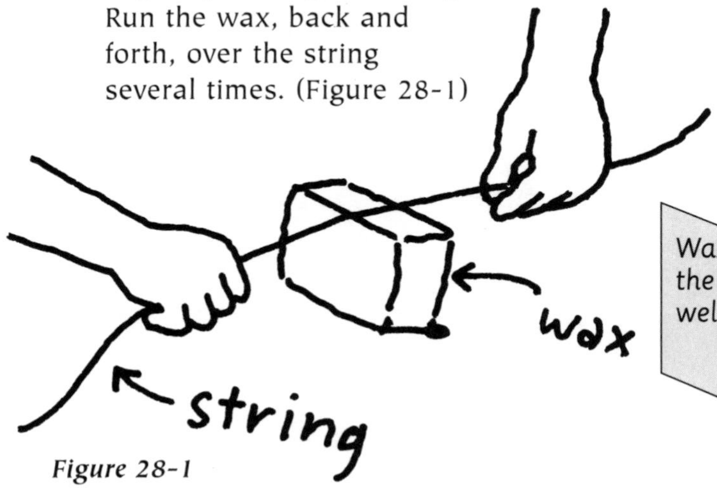

wax

string

Figure 28-1

Wax
the string
well.

You're making
dental floss for
a giant!

YOU NEED

Wax or paraffin

**String about
6 meters
(20 feet) long**

Nail

**Two same-size
Styrofoam drinking
cups or round
oatmeal boxes**

Two buttons

A partner

2 Carefully use the nail to make a small hole in the center of the bottom of each container.

3 Now thread one end of the string through the hole in one of the containers. Push the string through from the bottom, then pull it out the opening at the top.

4 Thread the string through a button and tie a knot. This is to keep the string from being pulled back through the hole.

5 Repeat the steps with the other container at the other end of the string.

6 Ask your partner to hold one of the containers while you stretch the string out taut, holding the other container. Be sure the string doesn't touch anything else.

7 Ask your partner to speak into the container he or she is holding while you listen in yours. What do you hear? Speak into your container. Can the other person hear you? (Figure 28-2)

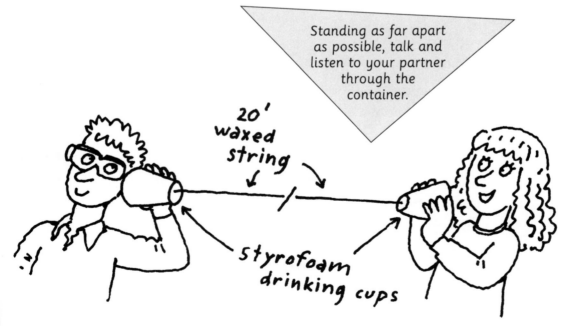

Standing as far apart as possible, talk and listen to your partner through the container.

20' waxed string

Styrofoam drinking cups

Figure 28-2

What Happened?

When you talk into the containers, the air begins vibrating. This causes the container to vibrate, which, in turn, makes the string vibrate. The string makes the other container vibrate. This experiment works best outside and away from any walls that might reflect sound.

Why do you think the sound is carried better if the string is waxed? How does this compare to a regular telephone cord? Try your phone again, but have your friend stand around a corner. Does your phone still work?

Check This Out

With a tape recorder, record the sound of bouncing a basketball in a room such as a gym. Then tape the sound of a bouncing basketball outside. How are the sounds different? What do you think causes this?

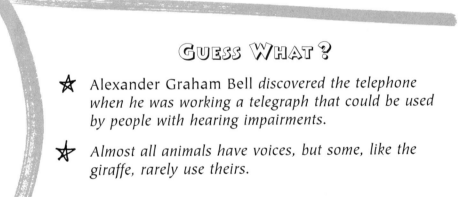

Guess What?

★ Alexander Graham Bell *discovered the telephone when he was working a telegraph that could be used by people with hearing impairments.*

★ *Almost all animals have voices, but some, like the giraffe, rarely use theirs.*

This experiment will mess with your head.

SOUND SENSING

YOUR CHALLENGE

To observe how sensitive our brain is in comparing sound levels to locate a direction.

DO THIS

1   Have your partner sit in a chair in front of you. Ask your partner to raise the left hand whenever he or she hears a sound coming from the left side, the right hand when the sound comes from the right, and both hands when the sound comes from directly behind your partner's head.

2   Begin testing by tapping the spoons together once about 30 cm (12 inches) to one side of your partner's head.

3   Next, tap the spoons together on the other side of your partner's head.

YOU NEED

Chair

Two spoons

Empty paper-towel cardboard tube

A partner

4 Tap the spoons directly behind your partner's head. Did your partner raise the correct hand when you tapped the spoons to the left or right side? Did your partner raise both hands when the sound was directly behind his or her head? (Figure 29-1)

Figure 29-1

5 Now, ask your partner to hold one end of the tube against his or her ear, while the other end sticks straight out to the side.

6 Repeat the steps. Is there a difference in the results? Where do they think the sounds came from? Take turns and see if you hear the sounds the same way.

WHAT HAPPENED ?

Our brain can measure the difference between the time it takes the sound waves to reach one ear and the time it takes for the waves to reach the other ear. In the first part of the experiment, the brain was able to estimate the distance between the two ears. This is how your partner knew where the sound was coming from. In the second part, the brain knew the distance between the open end of the tube and the ear on the opposite side of the head. This produced false information to the brain.

CHECK THIS OUT

You've probably put your ear to a seashell to listen to the "ocean." Do you know what you are really hearing? Here's a clue: The sound isn't *really* coming from inside the shell. The shell just works as an amplifier. In fact, you can get the same effect by holding an ordinary drinking glass to your ear. (Figure 29-2)

Figure 29-2

GUESS WHAT?

★ A stethoscope *allows physicians to clearly hear the sounds of a beating heart, as well as air passing through the lungs.*

★ *Your heartbeat is caused by the closing of heart valves and the contraction of the heart muscle.*

GLOSSARY

acoustics The study of how sound waves behave and the methods for controlling them.

amplify To make louder.

audio The frequency of sound waves that can be normally heard by the human ear.

Concorde A supersonic transport aircraft built by the British and French governments.

compress To squeeze together.

concussion A violent shaking from an impact.

dampen To lessen the sound of something by reducing vibrations.

decibel The numerical term used to describe the relative loudness of a sound. Abbreviated dB.

Doppler, Christian Johann (1803–1853) Austrian physicist who discovered the Doppler effect.

Doppler effect The apparent change of frequencies of sound waves or light waves varying with the speed and direction between the source and the observer.

eardrum   A thin, oval-shaped membrane that separates the outer ear from the middle ear. The eardrum receives the vibrations of sound waves. Also called the *tympanic membrane*.

echolocation   The determination of the position of an object by reflected sound waves.

frequency   The number of periodic oscillations, vibrations, or waves for a period of time: usually expressed in hertz.

Genghis Khan   (1162–1277) Mongol conqueror of central Asia.

geophysicist   A scientist that deals with the physics of the earth, including weather, winds, tides, earthquakes, volcanoes, etc. and their effects on the earth.

hertz   The international unit of frequency, defined as one cycle per second.

hydrophone   An instrument for detecting the distance and direction of sound transmitted through water.

inner ear   The portion of the ear that includes the cochlea and other semicircular canals. The inner ear is essential for hearing and balance.

instinct   An inborn pattern of behavior of a creature.

iron oxide   A material used to coat recording tape.

Krakatoa   A small island volcano between Sumatra and Java.

larynx   The structure of muscle and cartilage in the throat containing the vocal cords.

laser   A device that creates and amplifies a narrow, intense beam of light. The word comes from *l*ight *a*mplification by *s*imulated *e*mission of *r*adiation.

Mach number   A number representing the ratio of the speed of an object to the speed of sound: Mach 1 means that the object is traveling at the speed of sound; Mach 2 means the speed of the object is twice the speed of sound, etc.

membrane   A thin, soft skin of animal or vegetable tissue that serves as a lining or covering of an organ.

middle ear An air-filled chamber of the ear that includes three bones: the anvil, the hammer, and the stirrup. These bones transfer vibrations to the inner ear.

mixing To adjust the volume and tonal qualities of various tracks of a recording, combining them into a finished musical piece.

molecule The smallest natural occurring particle of a substance made up of one or more atoms.

nature versus nurture The debate among scientists about whether certain behaviors in creatures are learned or inborn.

outer ear The portion of the ear that we can see, along with the ear canal.

overtone Any of the higher tones heard that has the exact multiple of the frequency of the original tone.

pitch That element of a sound or tone determined by the frequency of the sound waves reaching the ear: the higher the frequency, the higher the pitch.

resonance The reinforcement and prolongation of a tone or sound by sympathetic vibrations from other vibrating objects.

seismic wave A shock wave caused by an earthquake or by man-made tremors.

shock wave A high-intensity sound wave caused by explosions on land or under water, lightning, or supersonic aircraft.

sonar A device that sends high-frequency sound waves through water and shows the vibrations reflected from an object.

sonic boom The explosive sound that results when the shock wave caused by an object such as an aircraft traveling at supersonic speeds reaches the ground.

sound channels Underwater channels that allow sound waves to be detected at great distances.

sounding A method to determine the depth of a body of water. The first sounding devices were simply a weighted line marked off at intervals, such as fathoms. When the weight hit the bottom of the body of water, the measurement could be taken. Today's sounding devices are echo sounders, which measure the depth of the water by sending out a series of sounds from the bottom of a ship. These sounds bounce off the floor of the body of water and are reflected back to the ship. The depth of the water is determined by how long it takes for the sound to return to the ship.

sound wave A pressure wave caused by some mechanical vibration that flows through a substance, such as air. Sound waves include waves within the audible range of the human ear.

species A class of creatures having certain characteristics in common.

stethoscope A hearing device used for examining the heart and lungs by the sounds they make.

supersonic Moving at greater than the speed of sound.

swim bladder An organ that certain kinds of fish use for balance.

sympathetic vibrations Vibrations caused by other vibrations at the same frequency from a nearby object.

syrinx The organ in the throat of a bird that allows it to sing.

tuning fork A pocket-size metal device, made of chrome, nickel, and steel, that produces a pure tone without overtones. Tuning forks are used as the standard by which to tune musical instruments.

ultrasonics The science that deals with mechanical vibrations above the range of human hearing.

ultrasounds Sounds too high for a human to hear.

vacuum A space where no air molecules are present.

vertebrates Any large animal including all mammals, fishes, birds, reptiles, and amphibians having a backbone and spinal column.

Wright, Frank Lloyd (1869–1959) United States architect.

volume The degree of loudness.

INDEX

124

ABOUT THE GUY WHO WROTE THIS BOOK

A keen observer of nature and an avid follower of scientific advances, author Robert W. Wood injects his own special brand of fun into children's physics. His *Physics for Kids* series has been through 13 printings, and he has written more than a dozen other science books. His innovative work has been featured in major newspapers and magazines.